The Daily Frisian Challenge

Learn 10 Frisian Words a Day for 7 Weeks

Introduction

Welcome to "Learn 10 Frisian Words a Day for 7 Weeks"! This book is designed to provide an engaging and effective learning experience for children and beginners who are eager to discover the beauty of the Frisian language. With its carefully curated selection of words and interactive approach, this book aims to make language learning a fun and enjoyable journey.

Learning a new language can be both exciting and challenging, but fear not! We have crafted this book with your learning needs in mind. Each day, you will encounter a set of ten Frisian words that are carefully chosen to be useful and practical in everyday situations. These words cover various themes, allowing you to expand your vocabulary and gain confidence in your language skills.

To facilitate your learning process, we have provided corresponding English words alongside the Frisian words, allowing you to establish meaningful connections between the two languages. By actively engaging in writing down (4x) the correct Frisian words, you will reinforce your memory and develop a solid foundation in the language. Embrace the joy of discovery as you unlock new words each day, steadily building your language skills one step at a time.

This book is meant to be your companion throughout the course of seven weeks, providing you with a structured learning experience. Each week is carefully planned to introduce new vocabulary while reinforcing previously learned words, allowing you to review and consolidate your knowledge. Make sure to allocate a few minutes each day to engage with the exercises and activities provided. Consistency is key, and your dedication will yield rewarding results.

Whether you are a young language enthusiast or a curious beginner, this book is designed to cater to your needs. The vibrant illustrations and interactive exercises are intended to spark your imagination and keep you engaged. Remember, learning a language should be an enjoyable experience, and we hope this book will ignite your passion for Frisian.

As you embark on this language learning adventure, we encourage you to embrace the challenge, celebrate your progress, and have fun along the way. Learning 10 Frisian words a day is an achievable goal, and with perseverance and dedication, you will unlock the doors to a new world of communication and understanding.

Happy learning!

Table of Contents

Week 1:

6.	Day 1:	Numbers
8.	Day 2:	Colors
10.	Day 3:	Family
12.	Day 4:	Food
14.	Day 5:	Animals
16.	Day 6:	Body
18.	Day 7:	Weather

Week 2:

20.	Day 8:	Months
22.	Day 9:	School
24.	Day 10:	Transportation
26.	Day 11:	Clothing
28.	Day 12:	Emotions
30.	Day 13:	Hobbies
32.	Day 14:	Sports

Week 3:

34.	Day 15:	Nature
36.	Day 16:	Days of the Week
38.	Day 17:	Music
40.	Day 18:	Jobs
42.	Day 19:	Fruits
44.	Day 20:	Vegetables
46.	Day 21:	Tools

Week 4:

48.	Day 22:	Kitchen
50.	Day 23:	Instruments
52.	Day 24:	Buildings

54.	Day 25:	Directions
56.	Day 26:	Bedroom
58.	Day 27:	Countries
60.	Day 28:	Travel

Week 5:

62.	Day 29:	Health
64.	Day 30:	Languages
66.	Day 31:	Church
68.	Day 32:	Birds
70.	Day 33:	Science
72.	Day 34:	Film
74.	Day 35:	History

Week 6:

76.	Day 36:	Drinks
78.	Day 37:	Business
80.	Day 38:	Beach
82.	Day 39:	Hospital
84.	Day 40:	Internal Body
86.	Day 41:	Internet
88.	Day 42:	Shapes

Week 7:

90.	Day 43:	House Parts
92.	Day 44:	Around the House
94.	Day 45:	Face
96.	Day 46:	Bathroom
98.	Day 47:	Living Room
100.	Day 48:	Finance
102.	Day 49:	Books

Week 8:

104.	Day 50:	Law

Week 1

Day 1: Numbers

One	Ien
Two	Twa
Three	Trije
Four	Fjouwer
Five	Fiif
Six	Seis
Seven	Sân
Eight	Acht
Nine	Njoggen
Ten	Tsien

Write the right words down twice on the next page

Six ....

Two ....

Eight ....

Four ....

Five ....

Eight ....

Seven ....

Three ....

Nine ....

Ten ....

One ....

Two ....

Ten ....

Four ....

Five ....

Six ....

Seven ....

Three ....

Nine ....

One ....

Week 1

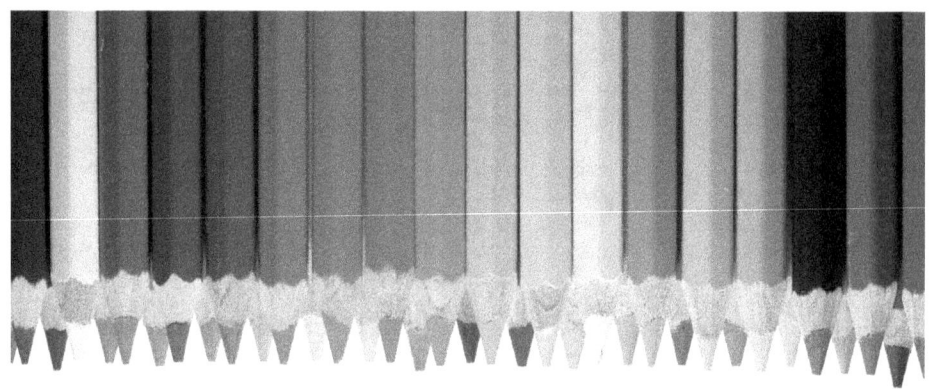

Day 2: Colors

Red	Read
Blue	Blau
Yellow	Giel
Green	Grien
Orange	Oranje
Purple	Pears
Pink	Rôze
Black	Swart
White	Wyt
Gray	Griis

Write the right words down twice on the next page

Red	....	....
Purple	....	....
White	....	....
Gray	....	....
Orange	....	....
Purple	....	....
Blue	....	....
Black	....	....
White	....	....
Gray	....	....
Pink	....	....
Blue	....	....
Yellow	....	....
Green	....	....
Orange	....	....
Pink	....	....
Red	....	....
Black	....	....
Yellow	....	....
Green	....	....

Week 1

Day 3: Family

Mother	Mem
Father	Heit
Brother	Broer
Sister	Suster
Son	Soan
Daughter	Dochter
Grandfather	Pake
Grandmother	Beppe
Uncle	Omke
Aunt	Muoike

Write the right words down twice on the next page

Aunt	....	....
Father	....	....
Mother	....	....
Uncle	....	....
Brother	....	....
Sister	....	....
Son	....	....
Daughter	....	....
Grandfather	....	....
Sister	....	....
Aunt	....	....
Grandmother	....	....
Uncle	....	....
Son	....	....
Grandmother	....	....
Father	....	....
Brother	....	....
Daughter	....	....
Grandfather	....	....
Mother	....	....

Week 1

Day 4: Food

Bread	Bôle
Rice	Rys
Meat	Fleis
Vegetables	Griente
Fruit	Fruit
Milk	Molke
Cheese	Tsiis
Eggs	Aaien
Soup	Sop
Dessert	Neigerjocht

Write the right words down twice on the next page

Cheese	....	....
Meat	....	....
Dessert	....	....
Vegetables	....	....
Fruit	....	....
Milk	....	....
Vegetables	....	....
Eggs	....	....
Soup	....	....
Dessert	....	....
Bread	....	....
Rice	....	....
Meat	....	....
Fruit	....	....
Milk	....	....
Cheese	....	....
Bread	....	....
Eggs	....	....
Soup	....	....
Rice	....	....

Week 1

Day 5: Animals

Dog	Hûn
Cat	Kat
Lion	Liuw
Sheep	Skiep
Pig	Baarch
Ape	Aap
Tiger	Tiger
Bear	Bear
Horse	Hynder
Bird	Fûgel

Write the right words down twice on the next page

Ape ....

Cat ....

Bird ....

Lion ....

Sheep ....

Pig ....

Ape ....

Tiger ....

Bear ....

Horse ....

Bird ....

Dog ....

Cat ....

Lion ....

Sheep ....

Pig ....

Horse ....

Tiger ....

Bear ....

Dog ....

Week 1

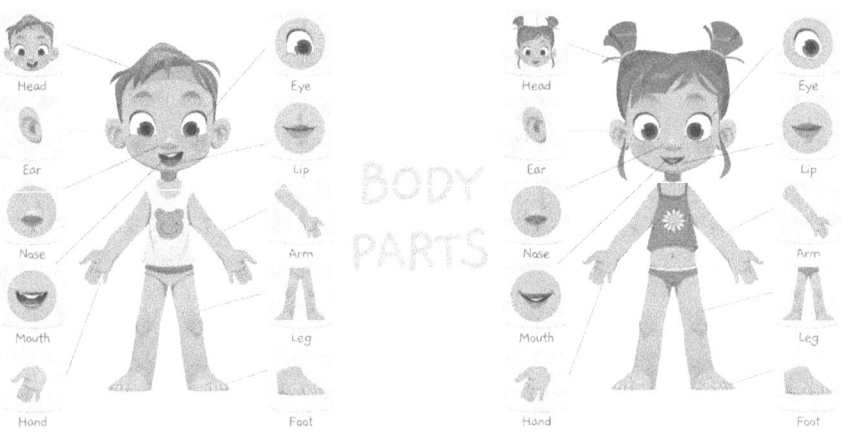

Day 6: Body

Head	Holle
Nek	Nekke
Belly	Búk
Shoulder	Skouder
Knee	Knibbel
Back	Rêch
Arms	Earms
Hands	Hannen
Legs	Skonken
Feet	Fuotten

Write the right words down twice on the next page

Shoulder	....	....
Back	....	....
Feet	....	....
Belly	....	....
Hands	....	....
Shoulder	....	....
Knee	....	....
Back	....	....
Arms	....	....
Hands	....	....
Nek	....	....
Feet	....	....
Head	....	....
Nek	....	....
Belly	....	....
Knee	....	....
Legs	....	....
Arms	....	....
Head	....	....
Legs	....	....

Week 1

Day 7: Weather

Sun	Sinne
Rain	Rein
Cloud	Wolk
Wind	Wyn
Snow	Snie
Thunder	Tonger
Lightning	Wjerljocht
Storm	Stoarm
Fog	Dize
Rainbow	Reinbôge

Write the right words down twice on the next page

Storm	....	....
Rain	....	....
Fog	....	....
Snow	....	....
Cloud	....	....
Wind	....	....
Snow	....	....
Thunder	....	....
Rain	....	....
Lightning	....	....
Storm	....	....
Fog	....	....
Rainbow	....	....
Sun	....	....
Cloud	....	....
Wind	....	....
Thunder	....	....
Lightning	....	....
Rainbow	....	....
Sun	....	....

Week 2

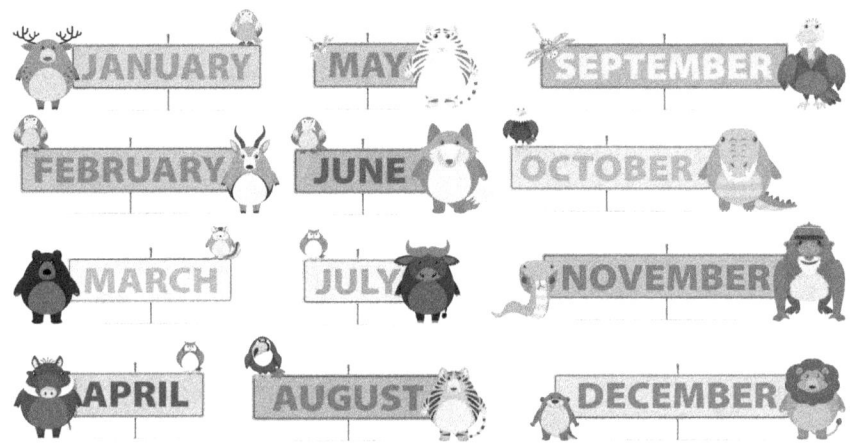

Day 8: Months

January	Jannewaris
February	Febrewaris
May	Maaie
June	Juny
July	July
August	Augustus
September	Septimber
October	Oktober
November	Novimber
December	Desimber

Write the right words down twice on the next page

October ……………………… ………………………

February ……………………… ………………………

August ……………………… ………………………

October ……………………… ………………………

April ……………………… ………………………

May ……………………… ………………………

June ……………………… ………………………

August ……………………… ………………………

March ……………………… ………………………

September ……………………… ………………………

May ……………………… ………………………

January ……………………… ………………………

July ……………………… ………………………

March ……………………… ………………………

April ……………………… ………………………

June ……………………… ………………………

January ……………………… ………………………

July ……………………… ………………………

February ……………………… ………………………

September ……………………… ………………………

Week 2

Day 9: School

Teacher	Dosint
Student	Studint
Classroom	Klasse
Book	Boek
Pen	Pinne
Pencil	Poatlead
Desk	Buro
Chair	Stoel
Homework	Hûswurk
Exam	Eksamen

Write the right words down twice on the next page

Chair	....	....
Homework	....	....
Teacher	....	....
Student	....	....
Classroom	....	....
Exam	....	....
Pen	....	....
Pencil	....	....
Desk	....	....
Classroom	....	....
Homework	....	....
Exam	....	....
Teacher	....	....
Student	....	....
Desk	....	....
Book	....	....
Pen	....	....
Pencil	....	....
Chair	....	....
Book	....	....

Week 2

Day 10: Transportation

Car	Lúksewein
Bus	Bus
Train	Trein
Bicycle	Fyts
Motorcycle	Motorfyts
Boat	Boat
Airplane	Fleanmasine
Helicopter	Giselwjuk
Truck	Frachtwein
Metro	Metro

Write the right words down twice on the next page

Airplane ....

Bus ....

Train ....

Metro ....

Truck ....

Motorcycle ....

Boat ....

Airplane ....

Helicopter ....

Truck ....

Metro ....

Car ....

Bus ....

Train ....

Bicycle ....

Helicopter ....

Motorcycle ....

Boat ....

Bicycle ....

Car ....

Week 2

Day 11: Clothing

Shirt	Sjirt
Pants	Broeken
Dress	Jurk
Skirt	Rok
Jacket	Jas
Shoes	Skuon
Socks	Sokken
Hat	Pet
Gloves	Moffen
Scarf	Sjaal

Write the right words down twice on the next page

Socks	....	....
Pants	....	....
Dress	....	....
Jacket	....	....
Skirt	....	....
Scarf	....	....
Shoes	....	....
Socks	....	....
Hat	....	....
Gloves	....	....
Scarf	....	....
Shirt	....	....
Pants	....	....
Dress	....	....
Skirt	....	....
Jacket	....	....
Shoes	....	....
Gloves	....	....
Hat	....	....
Shirt	....	....

Week 2

Day 12: Emotions

Happy	Bliid
Sad	Tryst
Angry	Lilk
Excited	Entûsjast
Surprised	Ferwûndere
Scared	Benaud
Nervous	Senuweftich
Bored	Ferfeeld
Confused	Ferbjustere
Calm	Rêstich

Write the right words down twice on the next page

Confused	....	....
Happy	....	....
Calm	....	....
Surprised	....	....
Sad	....	....
Angry	....	....
Excited	....	....
Nervous	....	....
Scared	....	....
Nervous	....	....
Bored	....	....
Scared	....	....
Calm	....	....
Happy	....	....
Sad	....	....
Bored	....	....
Angry	....	....
Excited	....	....
Surprised	....	....
Confused	....	....

Week 2

Day 13: Hobbies

Reading	Lêze
Painting	Skilderje
Singing	Sjonge
Dancing	Dûnsje
Cooking	Siede
Photography	Fotografearje
Sleeping	Sliepe
Writing	Skriuwe
Gardening	Túnje
Sports	Sporte

Write the right words down twice on the next page

Gardening ....

Painting ....

Photography ....

Painting ....

Dancing ....

Cooking ....

Photography ....

Sports ....

Writing ....

Gardening ....

Sports ....

Reading ....

Sleeping ....

Singing ....

Dancing ....

Cooking ....

Singing ....

Sleeping ....

Writing ....

Reading ....

Week 2

Day 14: Sports

Football	Fuotbal
Basketball	Basketbal
Tennis	Tennis
Swimming	Swimme
Volleyball	Follybal
Golf	Golf
Cycling	Fytse
Running	Rinne
Fitness	Fitness
Martial arts	Fjochtsport

Write the right words down twice on the next page

Swimming ....

Football ....

Fitness ....

Basketball ....

Golf ....

Swimming ....

Volleyball ....

Golf ....

Running ....

Cycling ....

Running ....

Fitness ....

Martial arts ....

Football ....

Basketball ....

Tennis ....

Martial arts ....

Volleyball ....

Cycling ....

Tennis ....

Week 3

Day 15: Nature

Tree	Beam
Flower	Blom
River	Rivier
Mountain	Berch
Lake	Mar
Beach	Strân
Forest	Wâld
Grass	Gers
Star	Stjer
Cloud	Wolk

Write the right words down twice on the next page

Grass	....	....
Beach	....	....
Mountain	....	....
Cloud	....	....
Flower	....	....
River	....	....
Mountain	....	....
Lake	....	....
Beach	....	....
Forest	....	....
Grass	....	....
Star	....	....
Forest	....	....
Cloud	....	....
Tree	....	....
Flower	....	....
River	....	....
Star	....	....
Lake	....	....
Tree	....	....

Week 3

Day 16: Days of the Week

Monday	Moandei
Tuesday	Tiisdei
Wednesday	Woansdei
Thursday	Tongersdei
Friday	Freed
Saturday	Saterdei
Sunday	Snein
Yesterday	Juster
Tomorrow	Moarn
Today	Hjoed

Write the right words down twice on the next page

Sunday	....	....
Tuesday	....	....
Saturday	....	....
Today	....	....
Wednesday	....	....
Tomorrow	....	....
Friday	....	....
Saturday	....	....
Yesterday	....	....
Tomorrow	....	....
Today	....	....
Monday	....	....
Thursday	....	....
Wednesday	....	....
Thursday	....	....
Friday	....	....
Monday	....	....
Sunday	....	....
Yesterday	....	....
Tuesday	....	....

Week 3

Day 17: Music

Song	Ferske
Melody	Melody
Rhythm	Ritme
Instrument	Ynstrumint
Singing	Sjongen
Band	Band
Concert	Konsert
Piano	Piano
Guitar	Gitaar
Sound	Lûd

Write the right words down twice on the next page

Concert ....

Melody ....

Rhythm ....

Sound ....

Guitar ....

Piano ....

Instrument ....

Singing ....

Band ....

Piano ....

Guitar ....

Sound ....

Song ....

Rhythm ....

Instrument ....

Singing ....

Band ....

Concert ....

Song ....

Melody ....

Week 3

Day 18: Jobs

Teacher	Dosint
Doctor	Dokter
Engineer	Yngenieur
Chef	Sjef
Police officer	Plysjeman
Firefighter	Brânwachtman
Nurse	Ferpleechkundige
Pilot	Piloat
Lawyer	Advokaat
Artist	Artyst

Write the right words down twice on the next page

Lawyer ……………………… ………………………

Teacher ……………………… ………………………

Chef ……………………… ………………………

Doctor ……………………… ………………………

Engineer ……………………… ………………………

Chef ……………………… ………………………

Police officer ……………………… ………………………

Pilot ……………………… ………………………

Nurse ……………………… ………………………

Doctor ……………………… ………………………

Artist ……………………… ………………………

Teacher ……………………… ………………………

Pilot ……………………… ………………………

Engineer ……………………… ………………………

Artist ……………………… ………………………

Police officer ……………………… ………………………

Firefighter ……………………… ………………………

Nurse ……………………… ………………………

Lawyer ……………………… ………………………

Firefighter ……………………… ………………………

Week 3

Day 19: Fruits

Apple	Apel
Banana	Banaan
Orange	Synapel
Strawberry	Ierdbei
Grapes	Druven
Watermelon	Wettermeloen
Pineapple	Ananas
Mango	Mango
Kiwi	Kiwy
Peach	Pjisk

Write the right words down twice on the next page

Orange ....

Apple ....

Banana ....

Orange ....

Mango ....

Grapes ....

Kiwi ....

Pineapple ....

Mango ....

Peach ....

Apple ....

Banana ....

Strawberry ....

Grapes ....

Watermelon ....

Pineapple ....

Kiwi ....

Strawberry ....

Peach ....

Watermelon ....

Week 3

Day 20: Vegetables

Carrot	Woartel
Tomato	Tomaat
Potato	Ierpel
Onion	Sipel
Cucumber	Komkommer
Broccoli	Brokkoli
Spinach	Spinaazje
Corn	Mais
Cabbage	Koal
Mushroom	Sjampinjon

Write the right words down twice on the next page

Corn ....

Tomato ....

Potato ....

Mushroom ....

Spinach ....

Onion ....

Broccoli ....

Spinach ....

Corn ....

Tomato ....

Mushroom ....

Carrot ....

Cucumber ....

Potato ....

Onion ....

Cucumber ....

Cabbage ....

Carrot ....

Cabbage ....

Broccoli ....

Week 3

Day 21: Tools

Hammer	Hammer
Screwdriver	Skroevedraaier
Wrench	Moerkaai
Pliers	Tange
Saw	Seage
Drill	Boar
Tape measure	Mjitlint
Chisel	Beitel
Shovel	Bots
Paintbrush	Fervekwaste

Write the right words down twice on the next page

Shovel ....

Screwdriver ....

Wrench ....

Paintbrush ....

Pliers ....

Drill ....

Chisel ....

Shovel ....

Paintbrush ....

Hammer ....

Screwdriver ....

Pliers ....

Saw ....

Drill ....

Tape measure ....

Hammer ....

Wrench ....

Saw ....

Chisel ....

Tape measure ....

Week 4

Day 22: Kitchen

Plate	Board
Fork	Foarke
Knife	Mês
Spoon	Leppel
Cup	Kop
Bowl	Kom
Pan	Panne
Pot	Pot
Cutting board	Snijplanke
Oven	Ûne

Write the right words down twice on the next page

Plate ....

Oven ....

Fork ....

Bowl ....

Knife ....

Spoon ....

Cup ....

Cutting board ....

Knife ....

Fork ....

Bowl ....

Spoon ....

Pan ....

Pot ....

Cutting board ....

Oven ....

Pot ....

Plate ....

Cup ....

Pan ....

Week 4

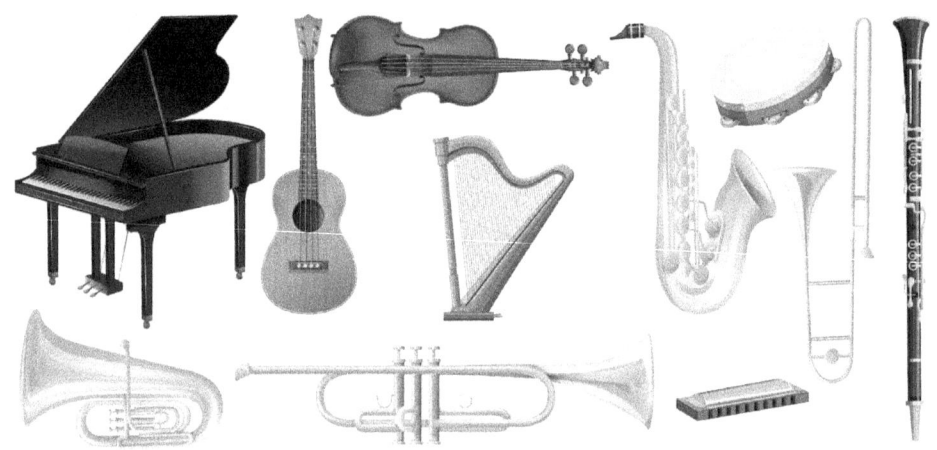

Day 23: Instruments

Guitar	Gitaar
Piano	Piano
Violin	Fioele
Flute	Floite
Trumpet	Trompet
Drum	Drumstel
Saxophone	Saksofoan
Cello	Sello
Clarinet	Klarinet
Harp	Harpe

Write the right words down twice on the next page

Flute	....	....
Piano	....	....
Trumpet	....	....
Violin	....	....
Cello	....	....
Trumpet	....	....
Drum	....	....
Saxophone	....	....
Cello	....	....
Clarinet	....	....
Violin	....	....
Saxophone	....	....
Harp	....	....
Guitar	....	....
Drum	....	....
Piano	....	....
Harp	....	....
Flute	....	....
Guitar	....	....
Clarinet	....	....

Week 4

Day 24: Buildings

House	Hûs
School	Skoalle
Hospital	Sikehûs
Library	Boekhûs
Bank	Bank
Restaurant	Restaurant
Hotel	Hotel
Museum	Museum
Church	Tsjerke
Stadium	Stadion

Write the right words down twice on the next page

Hospital	....	....
House	....	....
Museum	....	....
School	....	....
Stadium	....	....
Hospital	....	....
Church	....	....
Restaurant	....	....
Hotel	....	....
Museum	....	....
Church	....	....
House	....	....
School	....	....
Library	....	....
Bank	....	....
Restaurant	....	....
Hotel	....	....
Library	....	....
Bank	....	....
Stadium	....	....

Week 4

Day 25: Directions

Left	Lofts
Right	Rjochts
Straight	Rjocht
Up	Op
Down	Del
North	Noard
South	Súd
East	East
West	West
Stop	Stopje

Write the right words down twice on the next page

Straight	....	....
Left	....	....
South	....	....
Straight	....	....
Up	....	....
Down	....	....
North	....	....
Stop	....	....
East	....	....
Stop	....	....
Left	....	....
Right	....	....
South	....	....
Right	....	....
North	....	....
West	....	....
Up	....	....
Down	....	....
East	....	....
West	....	....

Week 4

Day 26: Bedroom

Bed	Bêd
Pillow	Kessen
Blanket	Tekken
Wardrobe	Kleankast
Nightstand	Nachtkast
Lamp	Lampe
Alarm clock	Wekker
Dresser	Kast
Hanger	Hinger
Mirror	Spegel

Write the right words down twice on the next page

Hanger	....	....
Pillow	....	....
Dresser	....	....
Wardrobe	....	....
Mirror	....	....
Nightstand	....	....
Lamp	....	....
Alarm clock	....	....
Dresser	....	....
Blanket	....	....
Hanger	....	....
Mirror	....	....
Wardrobe	....	....
Nightstand	....	....
Bed	....	....
Blanket	....	....
Lamp	....	....
Bed	....	....
Alarm clock	....	....
Pillow	....	....

Week 4

Day 27: Countries

United States	Feriene Steaten
United Kingdom	Feriene Keninkryk
Canada	Kanada
Australia	Austraalje
Germany	Dútslân
France	Frankryk
China	Sjina
Japan	Japan
Brazil	Brazylje
India	Yndia

Write the right words down twice on the next page

China ....

United States ....

India ....

Canada ....

Australia ....

Brazil ....

China ....

Japan ....

Brazil ....

India ....

United States ....

Germany ....

Canada ....

Australia ....

Japan ....

United Kingdom ....

Germany ....

France ....

United Kingdom ....

France ....

Week 4

Day 28: Travel

Airport	Fleanfjild
Passport	Paspoart
Ticket	Kaartsje
Suitcase	Koffer
Hotel	Hotel
Sightseeing	Besjennings
Beach	Strân
Adventure	Aventoer
Map	Kaart
Tourist	Toerist

Write the right words down twice on the next page

Airport	....	....
Adventure	....	....
Passport	....	....
Ticket	....	....
Suitcase	....	....
Hotel	....	....
Sightseeing	....	....
Beach	....	....
Adventure	....	....
Map	....	....
Tourist	....	....
Airport	....	....
Passport	....	....
Ticket	....	....
Suitcase	....	....
Hotel	....	....
Sightseeing	....	....
Beach	....	....
Map	....	....
Tourist	....	....

Week 5

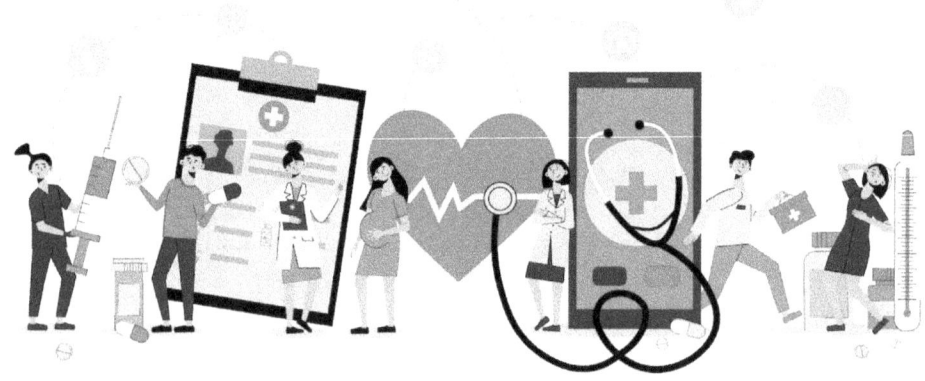

Day 29: Health

Doctor	Dokter
Hospital	Sikehûs
Medicine	Medisyn
Nurse	Ferpleechkundige
Pain	Pine
Appointment	Ôfspraak
Exercise	Oefening
Sleep	Sliep
Diet	Dieet
Vitamin	Fitamine

Write the right words down twice on the next page

Appointment ....

Vitamin ....

Hospital ....

Medicine ....

Nurse ....

Pain ....

Sleep ....

Hospital ....

Exercise ....

Nurse ....

Sleep ....

Diet ....

Vitamin ....

Doctor ....

Pain ....

Appointment ....

Exercise ....

Doctor ....

Medicine ....

Diet ....

Week 5

Day 30: Languages

English	Ingelsk
Spanish	Spaansk
French	Frânsk
German	Dútsk
Dutch	Nederlânsk
Frisian	Frysk
Russian	Russysk
Portuguese	Portegeesk
Japanese	Japansk
Italian	Italiaansk

Write the right words down twice on the next page

German	....	....
Spanish	....	....
Portuguese	....	....
French	....	....
German	....	....
Frisian	....	....
Dutch	....	....
Russian	....	....
Italian	....	....
Russian	....	....
Japanese	....	....
Frisian	....	....
English	....	....
Italian	....	....
English	....	....
Spanish	....	....
French	....	....
Dutch	....	....
Portuguese	....	....
Japanese	....	....

Week 5

Day 31: Church

Priest	Dûmny
Worship	Oanbidde
Prayer	Bea
Bible	Bibel
Sermon	Preek
Choir	Koar
Altar	Alter
Cross	Krús
Faith	Leauwe
Ceremony	Seremoanje

Write the right words down twice on the next page

Choir ....

Worship ....

Altar ....

Bible ....

Ceremony ....

Faith ....

Sermon ....

Choir ....

Altar ....

Cross ....

Faith ....

Ceremony ....

Cross ....

Priest ....

Worship ....

Prayer ....

Bible ....

Sermon ....

Priest ....

Prayer ....

Week 5

Day 32: Birds

Eagle	Earn
Sparrow	Mosk
Owl	Ûle
Seagull	Seefûgel
Hummingbird	Kolibry
Pigeon	Do
Flamingo	Flamingo
Swan	Swan
Peacock	Pau
Duck	Ein

Write the right words down twice on the next page

Duck	....	....
Eagle	....	....
Sparrow	....	....
Owl	....	....
Eagle	....	....
Swan	....	....
Sparrow	....	....
Flamingo	....	....
Hummingbird	....	....
Pigeon	....	....
Flamingo	....	....
Owl	....	....
Swan	....	....
Peacock	....	....
Duck	....	....
Seagull	....	....
Hummingbird	....	....
Pigeon	....	....
Seagull	....	....
Peacock	....	....

Week 5

Day 33: Science

Chemistry	Skiekunde
Biology	Biology
Physics	Natuerkunde
Astronomy	Astronomy
Experiment	Eksperimint
Laboratory	Laboratoarium
Microscope	Mikroskoop
Hypothesis	Hypoteze
Scientist	Wittenskipper
Discovery	Ûntdekking

Write the right words down twice on the next page

Hypothesis	…………………	…………………
Biology	…………………	…………………
Experiment	…………………	…………………
Astronomy	…………………	…………………
Physics	…………………	…………………
Astronomy	…………………	…………………
Microscope	…………………	…………………
Scientist	…………………	…………………
Laboratory	…………………	…………………
Physics	…………………	…………………
Microscope	…………………	…………………
Hypothesis	…………………	…………………
Chemistry	…………………	…………………
Scientist	…………………	…………………
Discovery	…………………	…………………
Chemistry	…………………	…………………
Biology	…………………	…………………
Laboratory	…………………	…………………
Discovery	…………………	…………………
Experiment	…………………	…………………

Week 5

Day 34: Film

Actor	Akteur
Actress	Aktrise
Director	Regisseur
Script	Skript
Camera	Kamera
Scene	Sêne
Drama	Drama
Comedy	Komedy
Action	Aksje
Television	Telefyzje

Write the right words down twice on the next page

Actor ....

Camera ....

Action ....

Director ....

Script ....

Television ....

Camera ....

Scene ....

Drama ....

Comedy ....

Action ....

Television ....

Actor ....

Actress ....

Director ....

Scene ....

Actress ....

Drama ....

Comedy ....

Script ....

Week 5

Day 35: History

Ancient	Skierâld
Civilization	Beskaving
Emperor	Keizer
Revolution	Revolúsje
War	Kriich
Kingdom	Keninkryk
Archaeology	Âldheidskunde
Renaissance	Renêssânse
Independence	Ûnôfhinklikheid
Event	Barren

Write the right words down twice on the next page

Kingdom ....

Event ....

Archaeology ....

Emperor ....

Renaissance ....

Independence ....

Revolution ....

War ....

Kingdom ....

Archaeology ....

Renaissance ....

Independence ....

Event ....

Ancient ....

Civilization ....

Emperor ....

Revolution ....

War ....

Ancient ....

Civilization ....

Week 6

Day 36: Drinks

Water	Wetter
Coffee	Kofje
Tea	Tee
Juice	Sop
Soda	Sûkerdrink
Milk	Molke
Wine	Wyn
Beer	Bier
Cocktail	Kokteel
Lemonade	Limonade

Write the right words down twice on the next page

Soda	....	....
Cocktail	....	....
Tea	....	....
Juice	....	....
Wine	....	....
Soda	....	....
Milk	....	....
Wine	....	....
Beer	....	....
Cocktail	....	....
Lemonade	....	....
Water	....	....
Coffee	....	....
Water	....	....
Tea	....	....
Lemonade	....	....
Juice	....	....
Milk	....	....
Coffee	....	....
Beer	....	....

Week 6

Day 37: Business

Entrepreneur	Ûndernimmer
Company	Bedriuw
Marketing	Marketing
Sales	Ferkeap
Product	Produkt
Customer	Klant
Finance	Finânsjes
Strategy	Strategy
Profit	Winst
Investment	Ynvestearring

Write the right words down twice on the next page

Strategy	....	....
Company	....	....
Marketing	....	....
Sales	....	....
Product	....	....
Customer	....	....
Finance	....	....
Investment	....	....
Customer	....	....
Profit	....	....
Finance	....	....
Investment	....	....
Entrepreneur	....	....
Company	....	....
Marketing	....	....
Sales	....	....
Product	....	....
Profit	....	....
Entrepreneur	....	....
Strategy	....	....

Week 6

Day 38: Beach

Sand	Sân
Waves	Weagen
Sunscreen	Sinnebrân
Swim	Swimme
Seashells	Skulpen
Umbrella	Parasol
Beach ball	Strânballe
Sunbathing	Sinnebaden
Surfing	Surfen
Picnic	Leechbydegrûnfrette

Write the right words down twice on the next page

Beach ball	....	....
Sunbathing	....	....
Waves	....	....
Sunscreen	....	....
Picnic	....	....
Swim	....	....
Umbrella	....	....
Beach ball	....	....
Picnic	....	....
Sand	....	....
Sunscreen	....	....
Swim	....	....
Seashells	....	....
Surfing	....	....
Waves	....	....
Umbrella	....	....
Seashells	....	....
Sunbathing	....	....
Surfing	....	....
Sand	....	....

Week 6

Day 39: Hospital

Doctor	Dokter
Nurse	Ferpleechkundige
Patient	Pasjint
Emergency	Needgefal
Surgery	Sjirurgy
Appointment	Ôfspraak
Stethoscope	Stetoskoop
Sick	Siik
Medicine	Medisyn
Recovery	Oansterkje

Write the right words down twice on the next page

Nurse	....	....
Doctor	....	....
Appointment	....	....
Stethoscope	....	....
Emergency	....	....
Recovery	....	....
Nurse	....	....
Patient	....	....
Emergency	....	....
Surgery	....	....
Appointment	....	....
Stethoscope	....	....
Sick	....	....
Medicine	....	....
Recovery	....	....
Doctor	....	....
Surgery	....	....
Patient	....	....
Sick	....	....
Medicine	....	....

Week 6

Day 40: Internal Body

Heart	Hert
Lungs	Longen
Stomach	Mage
Liver	Lever
Kidneys	Nieren
Brain	Harsens
Intestines	Terms
Bladder	Blaas
Bones	Bonken
Muscles	Spieren

Write the right words down twice on the next page

Kidneys ....

Stomach ....

Heart ....

Intestines ....

Brain ....

Lungs ....

Stomach ....

Liver ....

Muscles ....

Kidneys ....

Intestines ....

Bladder ....

Bones ....

Muscles ....

Heart ....

Lungs ....

Bones ....

Liver ....

Brain ....

Bladder ....

Week 6

Day 41: Internet

Website	Webside
Email	Eamel
Social media	Sosjale media
Online shopping	Online winkelje
Search engine	Sykmasine
Password	Wachtwurd
Wi-Fi	Wi-Fi
Download	Delhelje
Upload	Oplade
Browser	Browser

Write the right words down twice on the next page

Browser	....	....
Website	....	....
Email	....	....
Social media	....	....
Wi-Fi	....	....
Search engine	....	....
Password	....	....
Wi-Fi	....	....
Download	....	....
Upload	....	....
Browser	....	....
Online shopping	....	....
Email	....	....
Social media	....	....
Online shopping	....	....
Password	....	....
Website	....	....
Download	....	....
Upload	....	....
Search engine	....	....

Week 6

Day 42: Shapes

Cirkel	Sirkel
Square	Fjouwerkant
Rectangle	Rjochthoeke
Triangle	Trijehoeke
Oval	Ovaal
Pyramid	Piramide
Cube	Kubus
Arrow	Pylk
Star	Stjer
Cylinder	Silinder

Write the right words down twice on the next page

Rectangle ....

Triangle ....

Pyramid ....

Arrow ....

Star ....

Cylinder ....

Oval ....

Square ....

Star ....

Cube ....

Cirkel ....

Pyramid ....

Cylinder ....

Cirkel ....

Square ....

Rectangle ....

Triangle ....

Oval ....

Cube ....

Arrow ....

Week 7

Day 43: House Parts

Roof	Dak
Door	Doar
Window	Finster
Floor	Flier
Wall	Muorre
Ceiling	Plafond
Stairs	Treppe
Bathroom	Badkeamer
Kitchen	Keuken
Bedroom	Sliepkeamer

Write the right words down twice on the next page

Wall	....	....
Door	....	....
Stairs	....	....
Ceiling	....	....
Floor	....	....
Wall	....	....
Ceiling	....	....
Bedroom	....	....
Stairs	....	....
Bathroom	....	....
Kitchen	....	....
Bedroom	....	....
Roof	....	....
Door	....	....
Window	....	....
Floor	....	....
Roof	....	....
Bathroom	....	....
Kitchen	....	....
Window	....	....

Week 7

Day 44: Around the House

Plant	Plant
Watering can	Jitter
Shed	Skuorre
Doorbell	Doarbelle
Fence	Hikke
Mailbox	Brievebus
Lawn mower	Gersmeaner
Wheelbarrow	Kroade
Shovel	Bots
Bench	Bank

Write the right words down twice on the next page

Watering can	....	....
Shed	....	....
Doorbell	....	....
Mailbox	....	....
Bench	....	....
Fence	....	....
Wheelbarrow	....	....
Shed	....	....
Mailbox	....	....
Bench	....	....
Lawn mower	....	....
Wheelbarrow	....	....
Shovel	....	....
Plant	....	....
Watering can	....	....
Doorbell	....	....
Fence	....	....
Lawn mower	....	....
Shovel	....	....
Plant	....	....

Week 7

Day 45: Face

Eyes	Eagen
Nose	Noas
Mouth	Mûle
Ears	Earen
Cheeks	Wangen
Forehead	Foarholle
Chin	Kin
Lips	Lippen
Teeth	Tosken
Eyebrows	Eachbrauwen

Write the right words down twice on the next page

Eyebrows	…………………………	…………………………
Nose	…………………………	…………………………
Chin	…………………………	…………………………
Forehead	…………………………	…………………………
Ears	…………………………	…………………………
Cheeks	…………………………	…………………………
Forehead	…………………………	…………………………
Chin	…………………………	…………………………
Nose	…………………………	…………………………
Lips	…………………………	…………………………
Teeth	…………………………	…………………………
Eyebrows	…………………………	…………………………
Eyes	…………………………	…………………………
Lips	…………………………	…………………………
Teeth	…………………………	…………………………
Mouth	…………………………	…………………………
Ears	…………………………	…………………………
Mouth	…………………………	…………………………
Cheeks	…………………………	…………………………
Eyes	…………………………	…………………………

Week 7

Day 46: Bathroom

Sink	Wasktafel
Toilet	Húske
Shower	Dûs
Bathtub	Bad
Mirror	Spegel
Towel	Handoek
Soap	Sjippe
Toothbrush	Toskeboarstel
Shampoo	Sjampoo
Hairdryer	Hierdrûger

Write the right words down twice on the next page

Mirror ....

Sink ....

Hairdryer ....

Shower ....

Bathtub ....

Mirror ....

Towel ....

Soap ....

Toothbrush ....

Toilet ....

Shampoo ....

Towel ....

Soap ....

Hairdryer ....

Sink ....

Toilet ....

Shower ....

Bathtub ....

Toothbrush ....

Shampoo ....

Week 7

Day 47: Living Room

Sofa	Bank
Television	Telefyzje
Coffee table	Salontafel
Bookshelf	Boekeplanke
Lamp	Lampe
Rug	Kleed
Cushion	Kessen
Remote control	Ôfstansbetsjinning
Curtains	Gerdinen
Fireplace	Stookplak

Write the right words down twice on the next page

Rug ....

Sofa ....

Remote control ....

Television ....

Coffee table ....

Bookshelf ....

Lamp ....

Cushion ....

Curtains ....

Fireplace ....

Sofa ....

Television ....

Fireplace ....

Lamp ....

Rug ....

Cushion ....

Remote control ....

Curtains ....

Bookshelf ....

Coffee table ....

Week 7

Day 48: Finance

Budget	Begrutting
Savings	Sparjild
Debt	Skuld
Income	Ynkommen
Expenses	Útjeftes
Bank account	Bankrekken
Credit card	Kredytkaart
Interest	Rinte
Loan	Liening
Stock market	Effektehannel

Write the right words down twice on the next page

Savings ....

Loan ....

Debt ....

Income ....

Expenses ....

Budget ....

Income ....

Expenses ....

Interest ....

Loan ....

Stock market ....

Budget ....

Bank account ....

Credit card ....

Debt ....

Savings ....

Interest ....

Bank account ....

Credit card ....

Stock market ....

Week 7

Day 49: Books

Writer	Skriuwer
Page	Side
Table of Contents	Ynhâldsopjefte
Foreword	Foarwurd
Introduction	Yntroduksje
Front cover	Foarkant
Back cover	Efterkant
Text	Tekst
Title	Titel
Picture	Ôfbylding

Write the right words down twice on the next page

Front cover	....	....
Table of Contents	....	....
Title	....	....
Picture	....	....
Introduction	....	....
Back cover	....	....
Page	....	....
Foreword	....	....
Title	....	....
Text	....	....
Back cover	....	....
Picture	....	....
Writer	....	....
Page	....	....
Table of Contents	....	....
Foreword	....	....
Introduction	....	....
Front cover	....	....
Writer	....	....
Text	....	....

Week 8

Day 50: Law

Witness	Skriuwer
Justice	Side
Judge	Ynhâldsopjefte
Victim	Foarwurd
Perpetrator	Yntroduksje
Court	Foarkant
Evidence	Efterkant
Lawyer	Tekst
Crime	Titel
Government	Ôfbylding

Write the right words down twice on the next page

Perpetrator	....	....
Court	....	....
Justice	....	....
Evidence	....	....
Victim	....	....
Government	....	....
Judge	....	....
Victim	....	....
Perpetrator	....	....
Court	....	....
Evidence	....	....
Lawyer	....	....
Crime	....	....
Government	....	....
Witness	....	....
Justice	....	....
Crime	....	....
Judge	....	....
Witness	....	....
Lawyer	....	....

Help Us Share Your Thoughts!

Dear Reader,

Thank you for choosing to read our book. We hope you enjoyed the journey through its pages and that it left a positive impact on your life. As an independent author, reviews from readers like you are incredibly valuable in helping us reach a wider audience and improve our craft.

If you enjoyed our book, we kindly ask for a moment of your time to leave an honest review. Your feedback can make a world of difference by providing potential readers with insight into the book's content and your personal experience.

Your review doesn't have to be lengthy or complicated—just a few lines expressing your genuine thoughts would be immensely appreciated. We value your feedback and take it to heart, using it to shape our future work and create more content that resonates with readers like you.

By leaving a review, you are not only supporting us as authors but also helping other readers discover this book. Your voice matters, and your words have the power to inspire others to embark on this literary journey.

We genuinely appreciate your time and willingness to share your thoughts. Thank you for being an essential part of our author journey.